SELECTIONS FROM THE MOVIE

UKULELE

BOUBLIL AND SCHÖNBERG'S

Les Misérables

ISBN 978-1-4803-4033-6

ALAIN BOUBLIL MUSIC LTD.

EXCLUSIVELY DISTRIBUTED BY

HAL•LEONARD®
CORPORATION
7777 W. BLUEMOUND RD. P.O. BOX 13819 MILWAUKEE, WI 53213

www.halleonard.com

At the End of the Day

Music by Claude-Michel Schönberg
Lyrics by Alain Boublil, Jean-Marc Natel and Herbert Kretzmer

THE POOR:

At the end of the day you're an-oth-er day old-er.
At the end of the day you're an-oth-er day cold-er.

And that's all you can say for the life of the poor.   It's a
And the shirt on your back does-n't keep out the chill.   And the

strug-gle, ___ it's a war.   And there's noth-ing that an-y-one's giv-ing.   One more
right-eous ___ hur-ry past.   They don't hear ___ the lit-tle ones cry-ing.   And the

day stand-ing a-bout, what is it for?
win-ter is com-ing on fast, read-y to kill.

1.

One less day to be liv-ing.
One day near-er to

THE WORKERS:

dy-ing.

At the end of the day there's an-oth-er day
At the end of the day it's an-oth-er day

dawn-ing.
o-ver,

And the sun in the morn-ing is wait-ing to
with e-nough in your pock-et to last for a

rise.
week.

Like the waves crash __ on the sand, like a
Pay the land-lord, __ pay the shop. Keep on

storm that-'ll break an-y sec-ond, there's a hun-ger __ in the land. There's a
graft-ing as long as you're a-ble. Keep on graft-ing __ till you drop, or it's

reck-on-ing still to be reck-oned. And there's gon-na be hell __ to
back to the crumbs off the ta-ble. Well, you've got __ to pay __ your

To Coda ⊕

pay
way

at the end of the

day.

FOREMAN:
At the end of the day you get noth-ing for

noth-ing.
Sit-ting flat on your butt does-n't buy an-y

bread.
WORKER 1:
There are chil-dren ___ back at home.
WORKERS 1 & 2:
And the

chil-dren have got to be fed.
WORKER 2:
And you're luck-y to be in a job,
WOMAN:
and in a

bed.
ALL:
And we're count-ing our
D.S. al Coda
bless-ings.

Coda

at the end of the day.

I Dreamed a Dream

Music by Claude-Michel Schönberg
Lyrics by Alain Boublil, Jean-Marc Natel and Herbert Kretzmer

I Have a Crime to Declare

Music by Claude-Michel Schönberg
Lyrics by Herbert Kretzmer and Alain Boublil

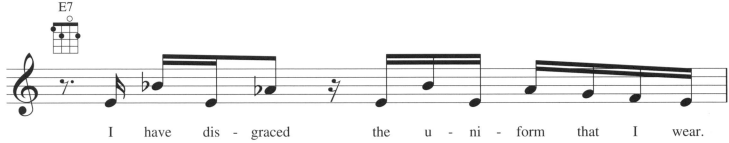

M' - sieur le Maire, I have a crime to de - clare.

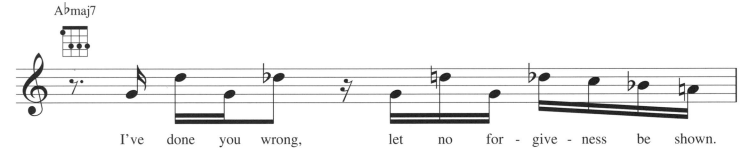

I have dis - graced the u - ni - form that I wear.

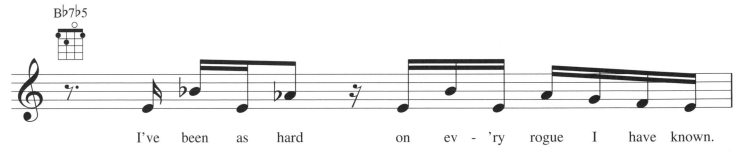

I've done you wrong, let no for - give - ness be shown.

I've been as hard on ev - 'ry rogue I have known.

I'll bear the blame, I must be treat - ed just the same.

VALJEAN: *I don't understand. What is this crime, Javert?*

JAVERT:

I mis-

took you for a con-vict. I have made a false re-port. Now I

learn they've caught the cul-prit, he's a-bout to face the court. And, of

course, the thief de-nies it, you'd ex-pect that from a con. But he

could-n't run for-ev-er, no, not e-ven Jean Val-

jean.

VALJEAN:

You say this man de-nies it

all and gives no sign of un - der - stand - ing or re - pen - tance? ___

You say this man is going to trial and that he's sure to be re - turned to serve his

JAVERT:

sen - tence? He will pay and so must I. Press charg - es a - gainst me,

VALJEAN:

sir! You have on - ly done your du - ty. It's a mi - nor sin, at most. All of

JAVERT:

us have been mis - tak - en. You'll re - turn, sir, to your post. Must I

VALJEAN:

do as you say? It's your du - ty to o - bey.

Stars

Music by Claude-Michel Schönberg
Lyrics by Herbert Kretzmer and Alain Boublil

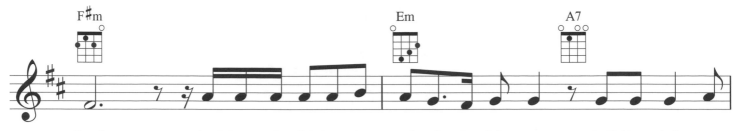

Lord.   And those who fol-low the   path of   the right-eous   shall have their re-

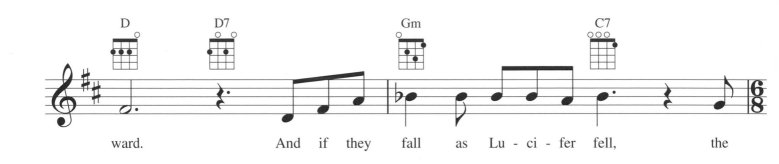

ward.   And if   they   fall   as   Lu-ci-fer fell,   the

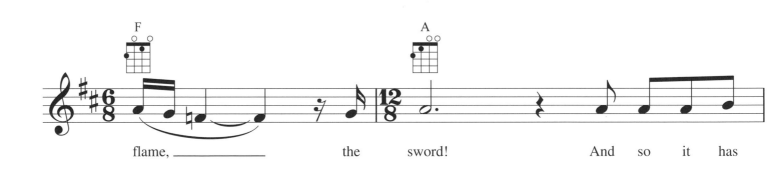

flame, ——————————— the   sword!   And so it has

been   and so   it   is   writ-ten   on the   door-way   to Par-a-dise   that those who

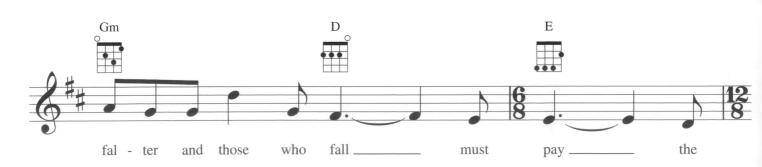

fal-ter   and those   who   fall ——————   must   pay ——————   the

price. _____

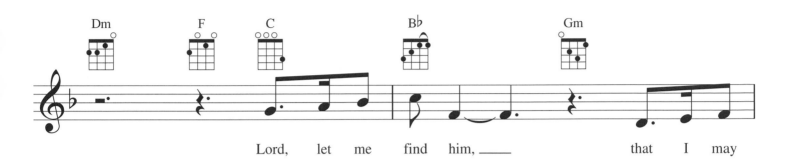

Lord, let me find him, _____ that I may

see him _____ safe be-hind bars. _____ I will

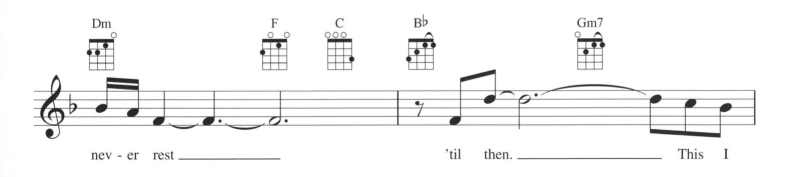

nev-er rest _____ 'til then. _____ This I

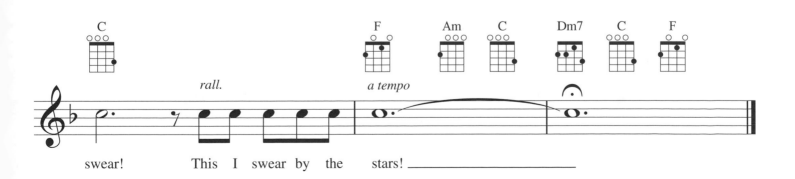

swear! This I swear by the stars! _____

Who Am I?

Music by Claude-Michel Schönberg
Lyrics by Alain Boublil, Jean-Marc Natel and Herbert Kretzmer

Castle on a Cloud

Music by Claude-Michel Schönberg
Lyrics by Alain Boublil, Jean-Marc Natel and Herbert Kretzmer

Master of the House

Music by Claude-Michel Schönberg
Lyrics by Alain Boublil, Jean-Marc Natel and Herbert Kretzmer

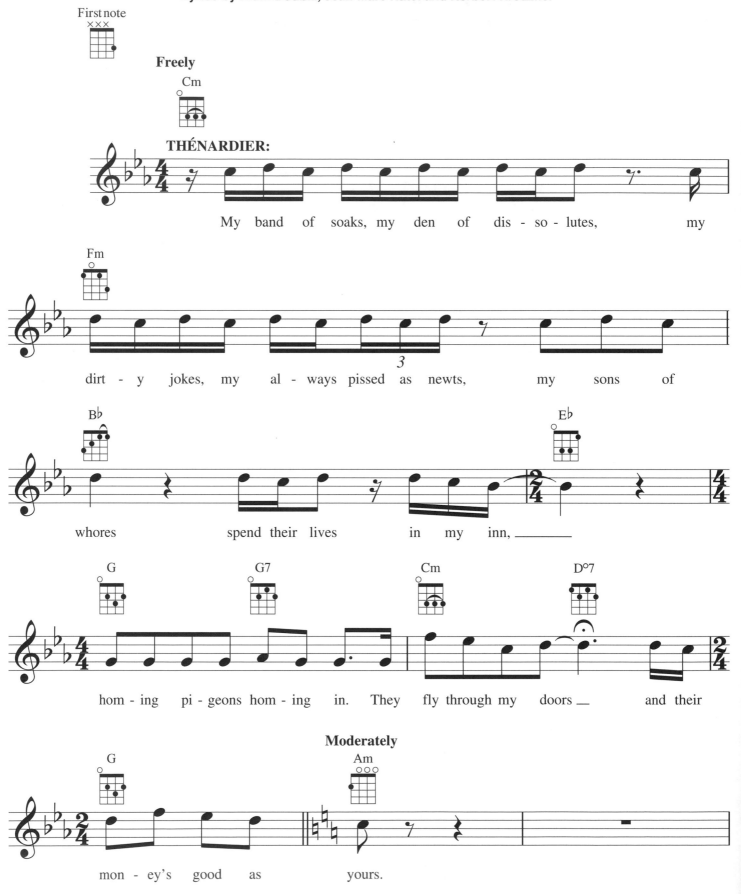

Wel-come, M'-sieur. Sit your-self down and meet the best inn - keep-er in town.

As for the rest, all of them crooks, rook - ing the guests and

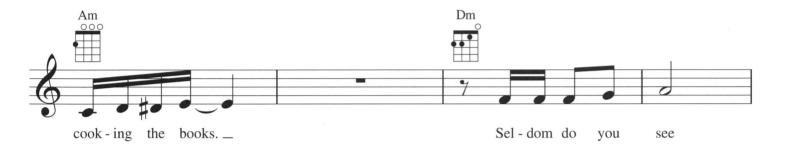

cook-ing the books. _ Sel - dom do you see

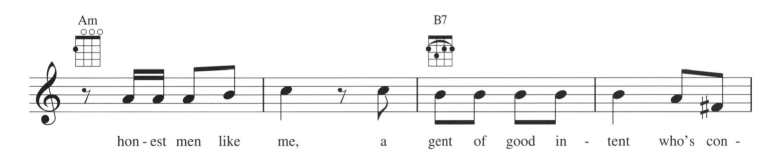

hon-est men like me, a gent of good in - tent who's con -

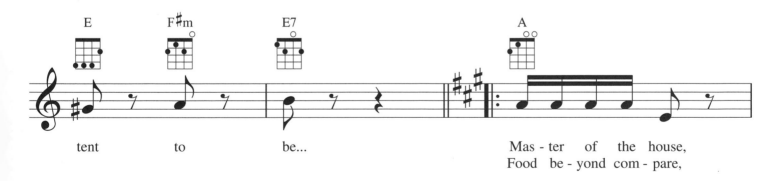

tent to be... Mas - ter of the house,
Food be - yond com - pare,

dol - ing out the charm, read - y with a hand - shake and an o - pen palm.
food be - yond be - lief, mix it in a minc - er and pre - tend it's beef.

Tells a sauc - y tale, makes a lit - tle stir, cus - tom - ers ap - pre - ci - ate a
Kid - ney of a horse, liv - er of a cat, fill - ing up the sau - sag - es with

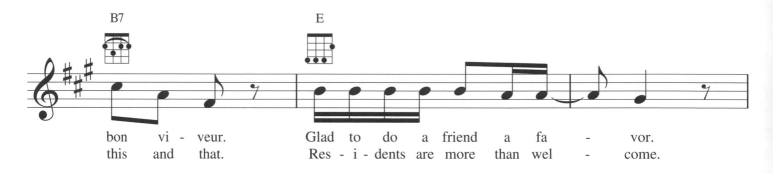

bon vi - veur. Glad to do a friend a fa - vor.
this and that. Res - i - dents are more than wel - come.

Does - n't cost me to be nice. ___ But noth - ing gets you noth - ing, ev -
Bri - dal suite is oc - cu - pied. ___ Rea - son - a - ble charg - es plus _

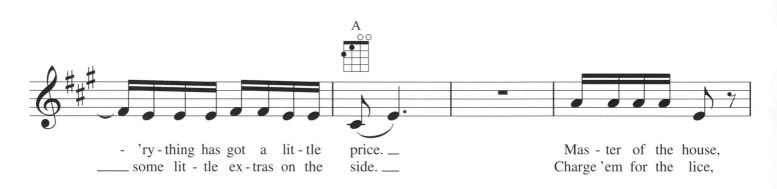

- 'ry - thing has got a lit - tle price. _ Mas - ter of the house,
___ some lit - tle ex - tras on the side. _ Charge 'em for the lice,

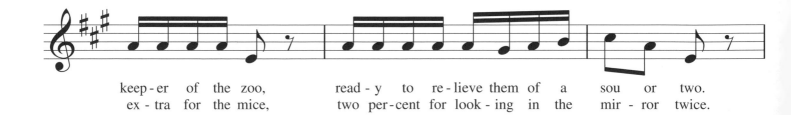

keep - er of the zoo, read - y to re - lieve them of a sou or two.
ex - tra for the mice, two per - cent for look - ing in the mir - ror twice.

Wa - ter - ing the wine, mak - ing up the weight, pick - ing up their knick - knacks when they
Here a lit - tle slice, there a lit - tle cut, three per - cent for sleep - ing with the

can't see straight. Ev -'ry-bod-y loves a land - lord,
win - dow shut. When it comes to fix - ing pric - es,

ev -'ry-bod-y's bos - om friend. _____ I do what-ev -er pleas - es, Je -
there are lots of tricks he knows. _

- sus, don't I bleed 'em in the end! _____

How it all in - creas - es, all _____ them bits and piec - es, Je - sus, it's a - maz-ing how it

Meno mosso

MADAME
THÉNARDIER:

rit.

grows! I used to dream that I _____

poco rall.

_____ would meet a prince. But, God Al-might- y, have you seen what's hap-pened since? _

23

Mas - ter of the house? Is - n't worth my spit!

Com - fort - er, phi - los - o - pher and life - long shit! Cun - ning lit - tle brain,

reg - u - lar Vol - taire. Thinks he's quite a lov - er but there's not much there!

What a cru - el trick of na - ture land - ed me with such a louse? _

_ God knows how I've last - ed liv - ing with this bas - tard in the

house!

THÉNARDIER & CHORUS:

Mas - ter of the house,

MADAME THÉNARDIER:

mas - ter and a half,

Suddenly

Music by Claude-Michel Schönberg
Lyrics by Herbert Kretzmer and Alain Boublil

Look Down
(Gavroche/Éponine new sections)

Music by Claude-Michel Schönberg
Lyrics by Alain Boublil, Jean-Marc Natel and Herbert Kretzmer

down   and show   some   mer - cy   if   you   can.   Look   down,   look down   up -

GAVROCHE:

on   your   fel - low   man. ____   There was   a   time   we   killed   the   king.

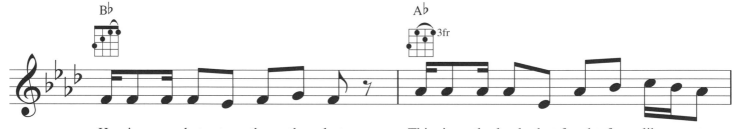

We tried   to change the world too fast.   Now we have got   an - oth - er   king.

He   is   no   bet - ter   than   the   last.   This is   the   land   that fought for   lib - er - ty.

Now when we fight, we fight for bread.   Here is   the   thing   a - bout   e - qual - i - ty:

Ev - 'ry - one's   e - qual   when they're dead.   Take your place,   take   your chance.

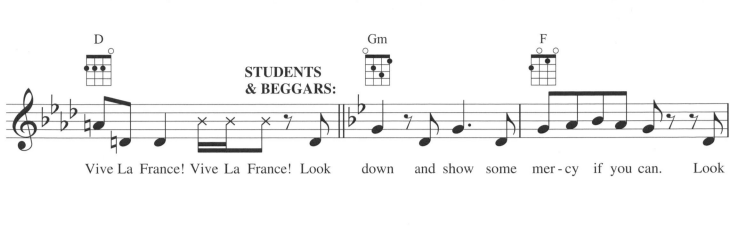

Vive La France! Vive La France! Look down and show some mer-cy if you can. Look

down, look down up-on your fel-low man. ___ When's it gon-na end?

When we gon-na live? Some-thing's got-ta hap-pen now,

some-thing's got-ta give. It-'ll come, it-'ll come, it-'ll come, it-'ll come, it-'ll

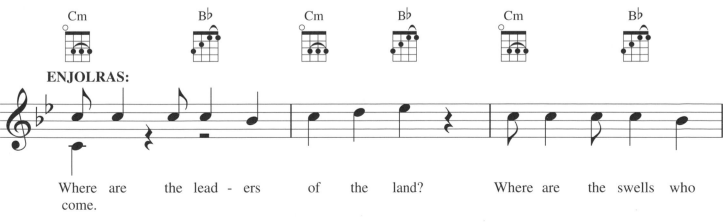

Where are the lead-ers of the land? Where are the swells who
come.

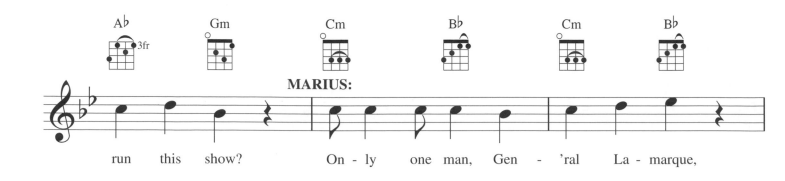

MARIUS: run this show? On - ly one man, Gen - 'ral La - marque,

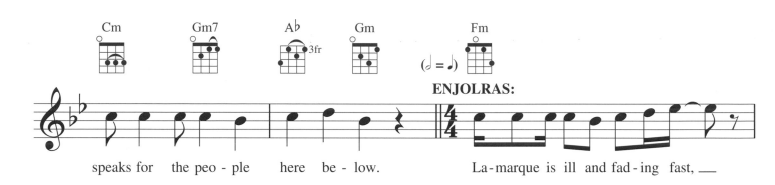

ENJOLRAS: speaks for the peo - ple here be - low. La - marque is ill and fad - ing fast, ___

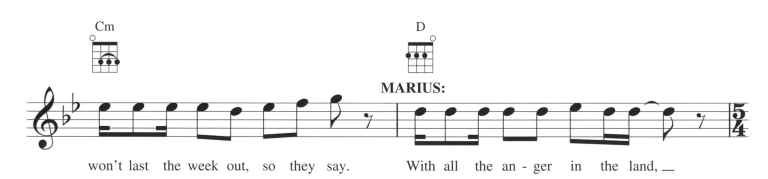

MARIUS: won't last the week out, so they say. With all the an - ger in the land, ___

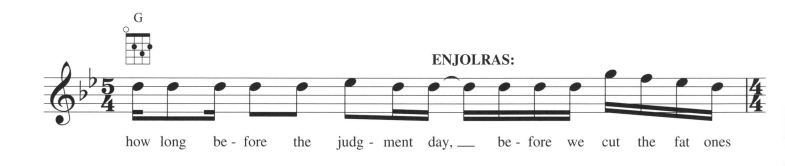

ENJOLRAS: how long be - fore the judg - ment day, ___ be - fore we cut the fat ones

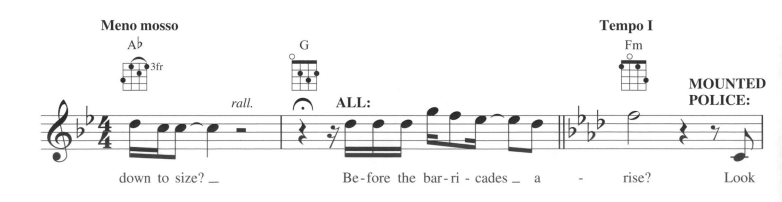

Meno mosso *rall.* **ALL:** down to size? ___ Be - fore the bar - ri - cades ___ a - rise?

Tempo I **MOUNTED POLICE:** Look

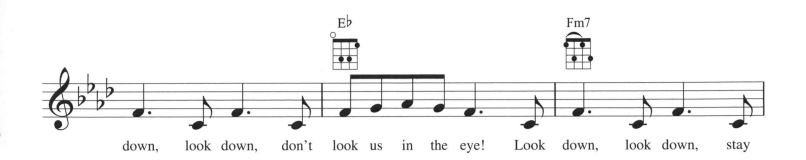

down, look down, don't look us in the eye! Look down, look down, stay

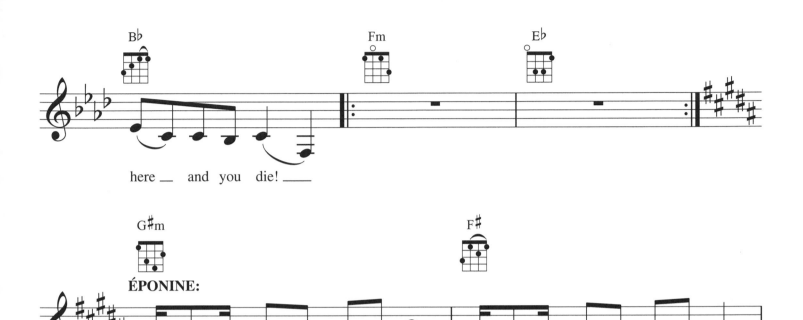

here __ and you die! ___

ÉPONINE:

Hey there, Mon-sieur, what's new with you? Have-n't seen much of you of late.

Plan-ning, no doubt, to change the world? Plot-ting to o-ver-throw the state?

Still liv-ing here in this old sewer?

Might as well doss down in a ditch. You still pre-tend-ing to be poor?

Ev - 'ry - one knows your grand - pa's rich.

MARIUS: *How did you…?*
ÉPONINE: *There's lots of things I know.*

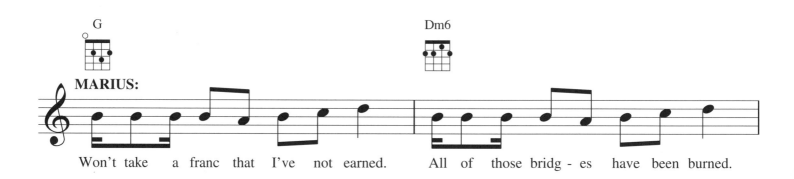

MARIUS: Won't take a franc that I've not earned. All of those bridg - es have been burned.

ÉPONINE: I like the way you talk, Mon - sieur, the **MARIUS:** way you're al - ways teas - ing me. ___

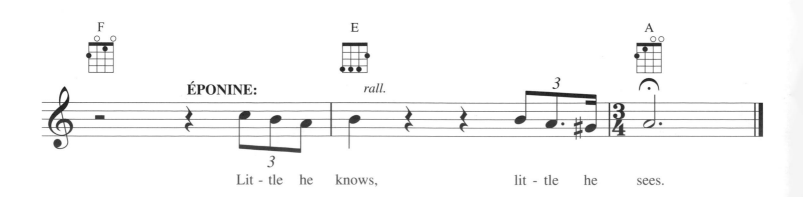

ÉPONINE: *rall.* Lit - tle he knows, lit - tle he sees.

On My Own

Music by Claude-Michel Schönberg
Lyrics by Alain Boublil, Jean-Marc Natel, Herbert Kretzmer,
John Caird and Trevor Nunn

mind,   that I'm talk - ing to my - self and not to

him.   And al - though I know that he is

blind,   still I say there's a way for us.   I

love him, ____ but when the night is o - ver, ____ he is

gone,   the riv - er's just a riv - er.   With -

out him the world a - round me chang - es.   The

Do You Hear the People Sing?

Music by Claude-Michel Schönberg
Lyrics by Alain Boublil, Jean-Marc Natel and Herbert Kretzmer

yond the bar - ri - cade, is there a world you long to see? Then
fall and some will live. Will you stand up and take your chance? The

join in the fight that will give you the right to be free!
blood of the mar - tyrs will wa - ter the mead - ows of France!

Do you

hear the peo - ple sing, sing - ing the song of an - gry men? It is the

mu - sic of a peo - ple who will not be slaves a - gain! When the beat - ing of your heart ech - oes the

1.

beat - ing of the drums, there is a life a - bout to start when to - mor - row

2.

STUDENTS & CROWD:

comes! Will you life a - bout to start when to - mor - row comes!

A Heart Full of Love

Music by Claude-Michel Schönberg
Lyrics by Alain Boublil, Jean-Marc Natel and Herbert Kretzmer

love.   No fear,   no _____ re -

gret.   **MARIUS:** My name is Mar - ius ___ Pont - mer - cy.   **COSETTE:** And mine's Co -

sette.   **MARIUS:** Co - sette, I don't know what to say.   **COSETTE:** Then make no

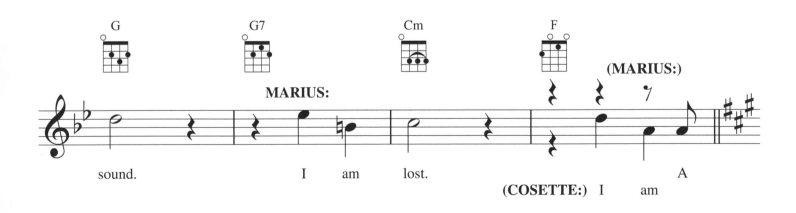

sound.   **MARIUS:** I am lost.   **(MARIUS:)**
       (COSETTE:) I am

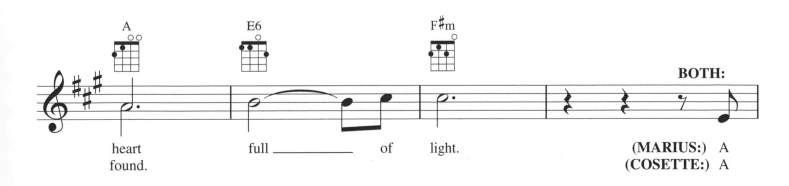

heart   full _____ of light.   **(MARIUS:)** A
found.   **(COSETTE:)** A

A Little Fall of Rain

Music by Claude-Michel Schönberg
Lyrics by Alain Boublil, Jean-Marc Natel and Herbert Kretzmer

past. And you will keep me safe. And

you will keep me close. I'll sleep in your em - brace at

accel. *più mosso*

last. The rain that brings you here

is heav - en blessed. The skies be -

rall. *a tempo*

gin to clear and I'm at rest. A breath a - way from

where you are, ___ I've come home from so far.

Drink with Me
(To Days Gone By)

Music by Claude-Michel Schönberg
Lyrics by Herbert Kretzmer and Alain Boublil

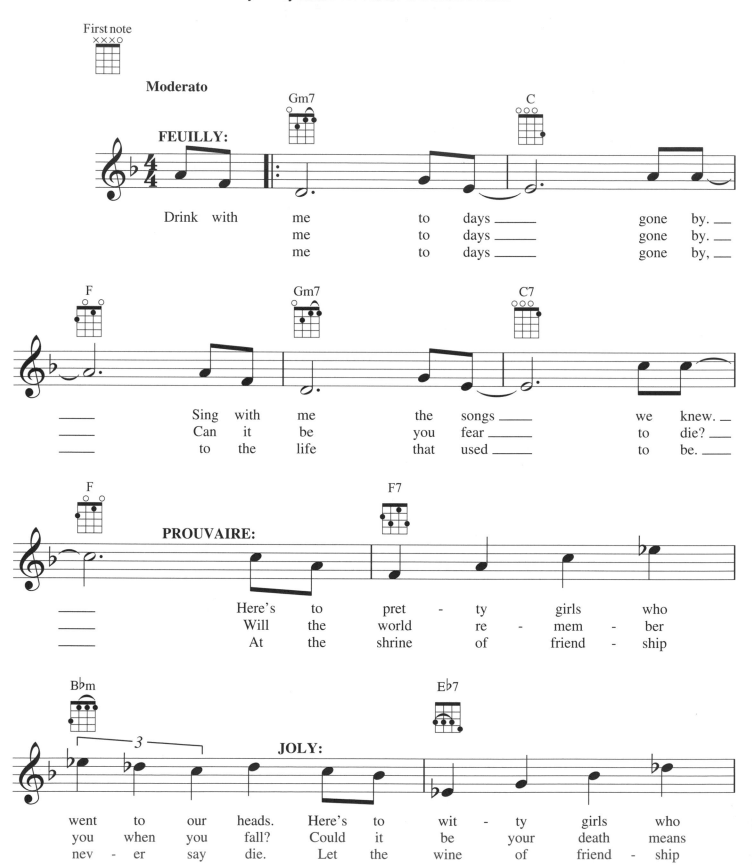

3 MEN:

went to our beds. Here's to them and here's to
noth - ing at all? Is your
nev - er run dry. Here's to

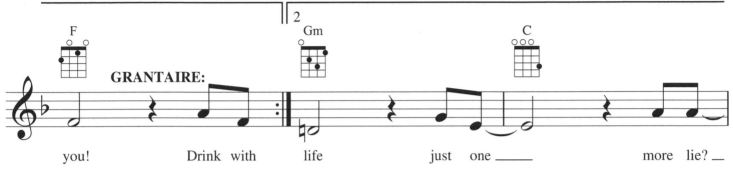

GRANTAIRE:

you! Drink with life just one _____ more lie? _____

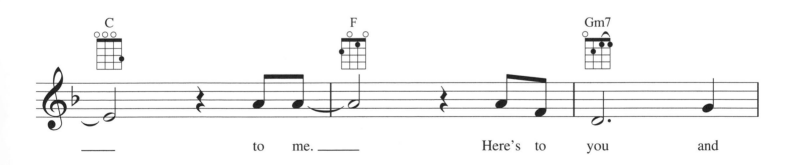

MEN:

_____ Drink with you and here's _____

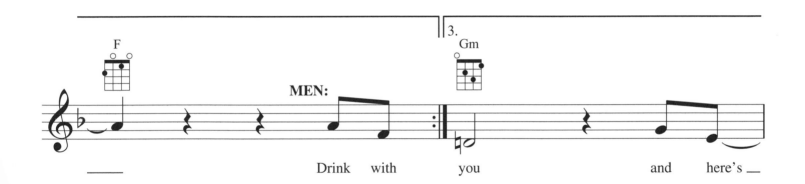

_____ to me. _____ Here's to you and

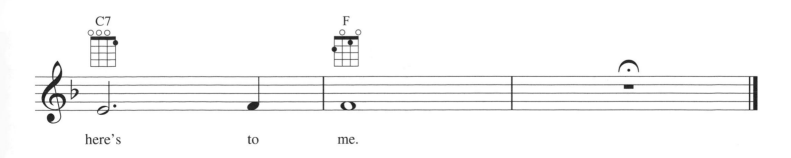

here's to me.

Empty Chairs at Empty Tables

Music by Claude-Michel Schönberg
Lyrics by Herbert Kretzmer and Alain Boublil

First note
Moderato

MARIUS:
There's a grief that can't be spo - ken. ____ There's a pain goes on and

on. _____ Emp - ty chairs at emp - ty ta - bles, now my

friends are dead and gone. Here they talked of rev - o -

lu - tion. ____ Here it was they lit the flame. _____

Here they sang a - bout to - mor - row, and to - mor - row nev - er

came.   From the ta - ble   in   the

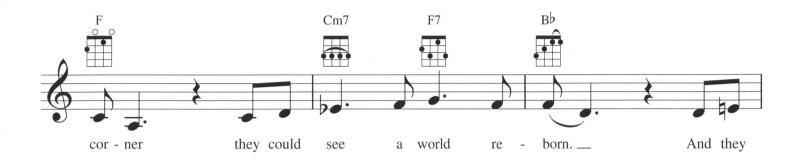

cor - ner   they could see   a world re - born. ___   And they

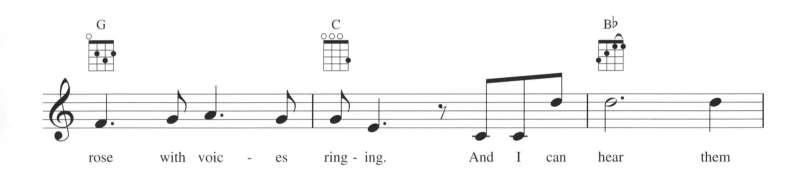

rose   with voic - es ring - ing. And I can hear   them

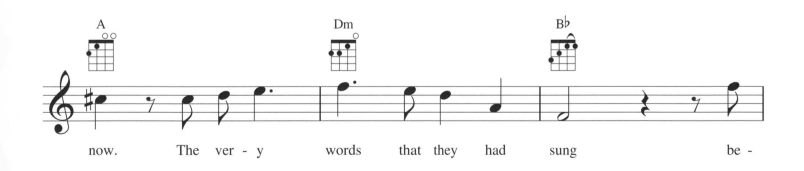

now.   The ver - y   words that they had sung   be -

come their last com - mun - ion _____   on the lone - ly bar - ri -

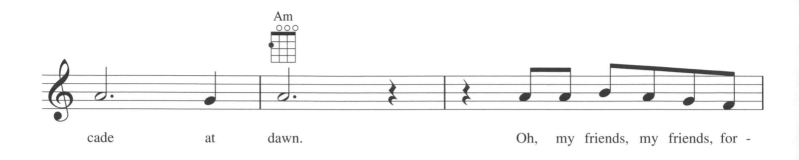

cade   at   dawn.   Oh,   my friends, my friends, for -

give me _____   that   I   live and you are   gone. _____

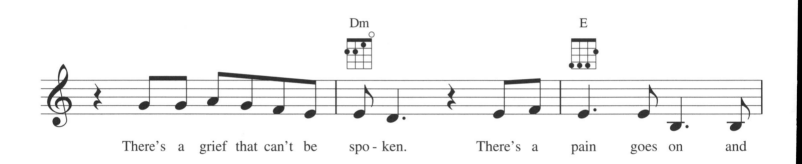

There's a grief that can't be   spo - ken.   There's a   pain   goes on   and

on.   Phan - tom fac - es   at   the   win - dow, _____

phan - tom shad - ows on the   floor. _____   Emp - ty chairs at emp - ty

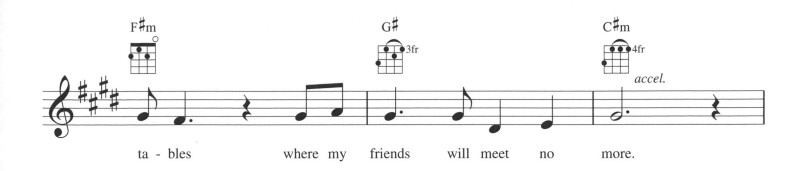

ta - bles where my friends will meet no more.

Oh, my friends, my friends, don't ask me _____

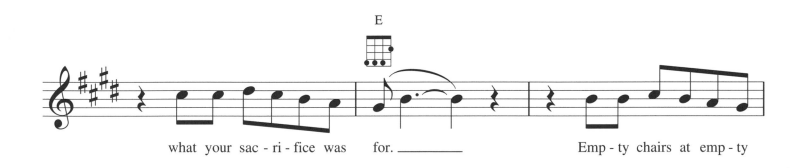

what your sac - ri - fice was for. _____ Emp - ty chairs at emp - ty

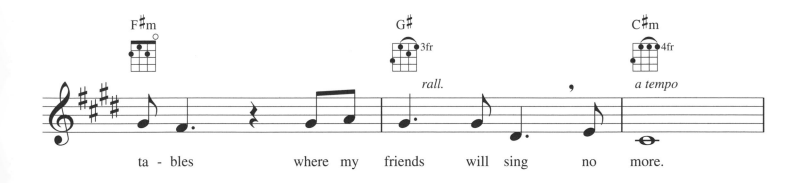

ta - bles where my friends will sing no more.

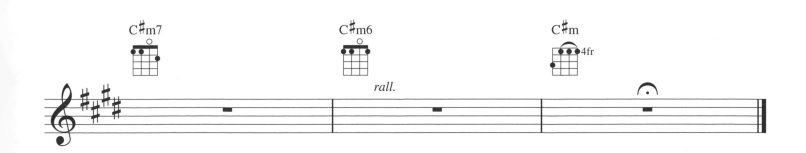

Bring Him Home

Music by Claude-Michel Schönberg
Lyrics by Herbert Kretzmer and Alain Boublil

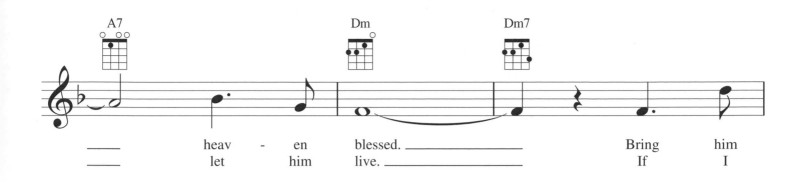

heav - en blessed. _____ Bring him
let him live. _____ If I

To Coda ⊕

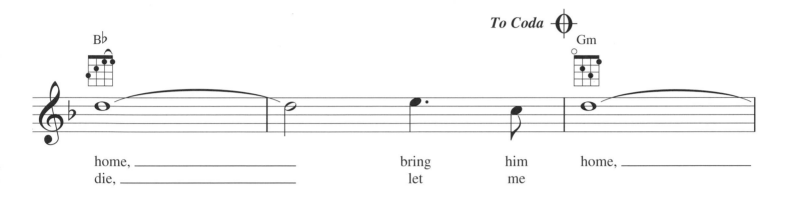

home, _____ bring him home, _____
die, _____ let me

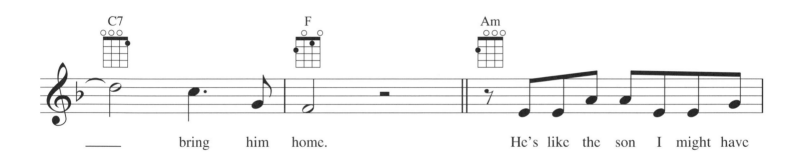

____ bring him home. He's like the son I might have

known if God had grant - ed me a son. The sum - mers

die one by one. How soon they fly on and

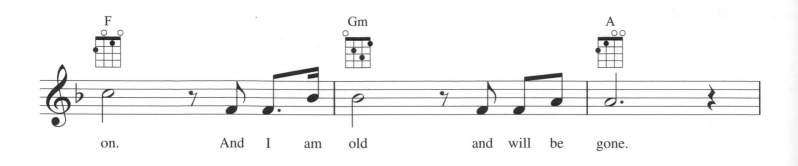

on.   And   I   am   old   and   will   be   gone.

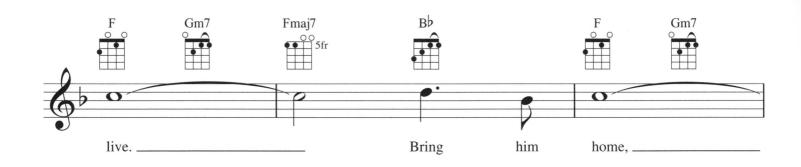

D.S. al Coda

Bring   him

Coda

die, _____   let   him

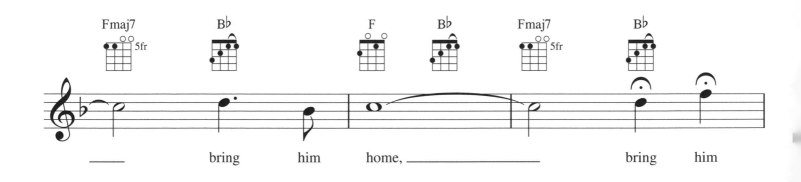

live. _____   Bring   him   home, _____

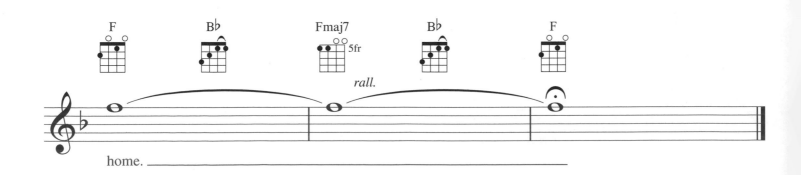

_____   bring   him   home, _____   bring   him

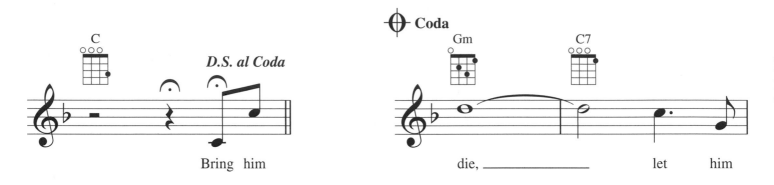

rall.

home. _____

56